Playground Fun

By Janice Behrens

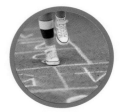

ISBN: 978-1-338-88853-9

Editor: Liza Charlesworth
Art Director: Tannaz Fassihi; Designer: Tanya Chernyak
Photos ©: JGI/Daniel Grill/Getty Images; 3: skynesher/Getty Images;
4: gpointstudio/Getty Images; 6: Kontrec/Getty Images; 7: monkeybusinessimages/Getty Images.
All other photos © Shutterstock.com.

SCHOLASTIC INC.

This is where kids swing.

This is where kids slide.

This is where kids dig.

This is where kids climb.

This is where kids hop.

This is where kids run.

This is where kids smile!